T0199021

Zoe's Gospel
HOPE

AMELIA SMITH

Illustrated by Rumar Yongco

WestBow Press books may be ordered through booksellers or by contacting:

WestBow Press
A Division of Thomas Nelson & Zondervan
1663 Liberty Drive
Bloomington, IN 47403
www.westbowpress.com
844.714.3454

Illustrated by Rumar Yongco

ISBN: 978-1-6642-0250-4 (sc)
ISBN: 978-1-6642-0251-1 (e)

Library of Congress Control Number: 2020915695

Print information available on the last page.

WestBow Press rev. date: 10/30/2020

WESTBOW
PRESS®
A DIVISION OF THOMAS NELSON
& ZONDERVAN

Zoe's Gospel
HOPE

"Granfoo, Granfoo who made the sky?

And who made me, Granfoo, and why?"

Oh, Zoe dear, come and sit by me

God gave you ears to hear and eyes to see.

God made the sky and everything

He made frogs hop and birdies sing.

He gave us His Word with the gospel story

It tells us of Jesus, the hope of glory.

God made you to be His child one day,

But the bad things we do- our
sin, gets in the way.

So, God gave His Son, Jesus
to be born as a man

To take away our sin, that's
God's great plan!

Oh, Zoe dear, the Bible
says no one is right.

We can't fix our sin, try as we might!"

"Even ME, Granfoo, even ME? Oh, No!"

"Yes, Zoe dear; Jesus,
He's our only hope!"

"God put our sins on Jesus when
on the cross Jesus died

God's love is SO big, SO
deep and SO wide!"

"Three days later, Jesus came
back to life: it's true!

Oh, Zoe, dear, He did that
for me and for you!"

"For the whole world, Granfoo,
for everyone?"

"Oh yes, Zoe dear, everyone who believes in God's Son!

God gives us faith to believe
and His Word is true

That's gospel hope, Zoe,
God's good, good news!"[1]

[1] *Scripture references: Col. 1:27; Jn 1:3,14; 3:16; Is.53:6; Rom 3:10-12; Rom 3:22,23; Rom. 5:5,6, 15:13; Phil. 2:5-8; Matt. 28:6*

Printed in the United States
By Bookmasters